Not My Dog

24 short stories that can change your life

Nancy DeYoung

Not My Dog: 24 Short Stories That Can Change Your Life
By Nancy DeYoung

ISBN paperback – 978-0-9844103-2-3

Printed in the United States of America

Contents

In this book, I have used the word "dog" as a metaphor for the responsibilities that we reject or accept into our lives.

Story 1
Not My Dog

> *"I have no dog in this fight."*
> IDIOM

It was an early fall evening when I joined my friend Shawn for a beer. As we sat at the bar in his garage, which he had converted into a man cave, we listened to "Iron and Wine" on the sound system and watched the sun sink behind Skyline Ridge through the open door. Shawn related this story.

My friends planned to visit the Black Hills in South Dakota for a family reunion. They rented a house for the week. I was very close to everyone in the family, so I anticipated seeing them several times during their stay.

Just days before the reunion, the Airbnb they had reserved fell through. At their last-minute request, I said they could stay at my house. The next day, Jonathan, Naomi, their two teenage children, and their dog arrived. We spent a

1

few days before the gathering getting back into our friend groove.

When the time for the family reunion arrived, Naomi's two sisters, Melanie and Joselin, and their mother, Jackie, came to get things ready. Eventually, the party grew to include the cousins, their children, and, more importantly, all their dogs.

When the crowd in the house reached 24 people and six dogs, I needed some quiet time and moved to the garage, which I had turned into a man cave many years before; it was my favorite place. Melanie, also a loner, joined me for a cigarette.

Melanie was from Tennessee and had come by herself, leaving her husband and dogs there. It was a beautiful day, and we had the garage door open, enjoying the fresh air (as we smoked our cigarettes). We were sitting on stools at the bar table, casually talking, when the door to the house opened, and all the dogs came rushing out past the person carrying the burgers to the grill. That person protected the burgers despite the dogs' ruckus as they rushed by. The commotion that ensued was characteristic of day-care children on too much sugar.

The people inside the house started yelling for the dogs, and although most of them went back in, one took off past our stools and out the open garage door. I stood to go after it, but Melanie sat perfectly still and took a calm drag from her cigarette. When I asked her if we should go after the dog on the loose, she breathed out the smoke, tapped the ash into the tray, and said, "Not my dog."

My shoulders dropped, and that frantic feeling of needing to do something quickly faded. I sat back in my chair and watched Joselin frantically run past us after her dog.

Darn right, it's not my dog!
SHAWN KRULL

When Shawn told this story, I laughed and laughed. It was similar to saying, "It's not my problem," or "It's not my job," but it felt different. Saying, "Not my dog," didn't seem as dismissive and added a detached lightheartedness. I liked it, and it gave me a new perspective.

Over the following weeks, I chuckled when I thought about Melanie's statement, but I also saw it as a guideline for making wise choices. By focusing on what belongs to us, we avoid unnecessary stress. Remembering this can help us look at situations that arise and ask ourselves if it really is ours to get involved. At times, we may conclude, "This is not my dog."

Metaphorical dogs include taking responsibility for cleaning up someone's mess, accepting criticism and unkind words, trying to solve another's problem, pleasing others, or allowing people to overstep our boundaries. When we claim ownership of any dog, be it four-legged or metaphorical, we make it ours until the dog dies, we walk away, or we renegotiate.

I'm not here to tell you what you should or shouldn't do but to point out circumstances that may no longer serve you. Keeping an open mind will help you let go of the old belief that you must be all things to all people.

The following stories are examples of situations that could be metaphorical dogs you have accepted. These accounts come from my life and those of people I know, but they are anyone's. As you read, take a moment to reflect on whether you have encountered similar situations and, if so, did you accept any that were not your dog?

The Takeaway: It's time to reevaluate the dogs in our lives.

Story 2
Just Dog

"Scratch a dog, and you'll have a permanent job."
UNKNOWN

When I was a child, Dad always had a dog that lived outside and slept in the garage; it was never allowed in the house. He never named them; he called them all "Dog." Dad had a gas station and auto repair shop, and our home was attached to it. Dog was there to guard the property, and he didn't want it to be overly friendly with people.

When my sister and I ran into the grain fields surrounding our ten acres, the tall grasses enveloped us; no one at the house could see us, and we could not hear them if they called. It was our place of escape. There was one dog that always ran along with us. We could only see the white tip of his tail above the weeds, so we called him "Tippy;" he was the first dog to have a name. He was always around. I liked him, but I didn't think much about him.

I have never felt the need to have a dog, but when I had children, they did, so after we settled into our new Colorado home, I relented and got them a French toy poodle. He was smart and didn't shed, so we got along well. After François died, we had another dog. He was a black mutt, and my daughters called him Boyshur. Don't ask where they got that name because I don't know, but it suited him.

My husband worked for an international engineering firm, and they transferred us to different construction sites in and out of the country. As a result, we traveled and moved often. A dog became out of the question, and I was okay with that.

After the kids were grown and my husband was no longer in the picture, I had a friend who cared for peoples' pets. She had so many jobs that she couldn't do all of them, so she passed some to me. For years, I was a professional pet sitter.

I liked this gig because it allowed me to spend time with dogs without a full-time commitment. I quickly learned which dogs were mine to care for and which were not. If a dog insisted on sleeping with me and repeatedly kicked me out of bed, I didn't go back. Similarly, if a dog pulled so hard on the leash that it jerked my arm and shoulder, I didn't return. I had many job offers, so I could choose the dogs I enjoyed.

Tending people's pets allowed me to travel and be with many amazing animals that I grew to love, but I was always clear about which ones were not mine. When it came to life's metaphorical dogs, I wasn't always so sure; that has taken longer to figure out. However, over time, I learned to recognize those too and can now confidently say, "This is not my dog."

The Takeaway: You can enjoy a dog without taking ownership.

Story 3
Naughty Dog

> *"Do you train a dog, or does it train you?"*
> UNKNOWN

Dogs and I have had a strange relationship. I like other people's dogs, but I want to avoid the everyday responsibility of having one. So, I have gotten my doggie fix from minding other people's pets.

One of my clients had an adorable 14-year-old miniature Australian Shepherd. I cared for her from the time she was very young; I loved that dog. When K.C. died, Lois wanted to get a puppy. I tried to discourage her as she was 88, and training a puppy seemed more than she could manage. Well, she did it anyway!

The breeder brought the tiny dog from Oklahoma to Santa Fe for Lois. She named him Sooner, and not being a sports fan, I thought that meant sooner rather than later. She educated me that people in Oklahoma are called Sooners, and since he was from there, he was a Sooner. Hence, that was his name.

Sooner was a toy Australian Shepherd and more of a challenge than Lois had anticipated. He grew and was no longer the cute little six-pound puppy she initially fell in love with. Now seven months old and twenty pounds, she could no longer lift him. He was naughty and still not potty trained.

Lois called at 6:30 one morning and wanted me to come to her house for a few days to care for him. Her heart had been in atrial fibrillation (A-fib) for the last day or two, and she needed rest. I agreed, which was not my first choice, but I didn't want her alone if her heart worsened. I was packing my things when she phoned and said that her friend had just called and said she was exposed to Covid the day before. She did not expect me to come and would make other arrangements. I was relieved.

One of my concerns was that if she did have Covid and went to the hospital, I would be

10

responsible for Sooner until she returned. I had a trip coming up, so I was grateful that she could make other arrangements.

After quarantine, she decided to rehome Sooner and thought I would provide that home for him. I suspected that question was coming and was glad I had time to think about it before she asked. I loved my apartment's serenity, cleanliness, and lack of clutter. I did not want to have piddle pads on the floor, urine in my carpet, be home at a specific time to feed him, get up early to walk him, or have to find a sitter when I wanted to go away for a few days. I didn't like the changes a dog, especially a naughty one, would bring to my home and lifestyle.

I knew the question was coming, and I knew how I felt, but what would I say? I cared for Lois and did not want to say no, but she had taken on this puppy. Was it my responsibility to carry it through?

In the past, I have said yes to many people's requests without thinking what that would mean for me. I have learned to say, "Let me think about that," which gives me time to decide the proper response.

It is much easier to say no initially because once we agree to something, we are stuck with the outcome or must renegotiate our role. There can be hard feelings if we don't amicably resolve the situation.

Determining what one's obligation is can be challenging. Some individuals know what they will accept, while others struggle to identify their responsibilities. If you are in the latter category, ask why you feel compelled to agree to tasks you don't want or don't have time to complete. By examining your feelings, you can better understand your role and speak up accordingly.

Addendum to the story:

Lois kept Sooner. She hired a trainer who helped Sooner fit into his new life and taught Lois how to work with him. He is now one year old, well-behaved, and has grown into the love of her life.

If I had agreed to take him, she would not have her little companion, and I would be miserable. Even though it was hard to say no, it was the right decision for all three of us. Sooner was not my dog.

The Takeaway: Do what you know is right; ultimately, it will be best for everyone.

Story 4
The Neighbor's Dog

"I don't think twice about picking up my dog's poop,
but if another dog's poop is next to it,
I think, 'Eww, dog poop!"

JONAH GOLDBERG

We have talked about literal dogs, but now, let's look at metaphorical dogs. I wondered what the consensus was concerning taking on obligations, so I asked an artificial intelligence (AI) program to write a paragraph about "it's not my metaphorical dog." Since AI draws from millions of websites, it gathers many peoples' ideas, which would give me insight into the collective opinion. The following is the reply I received.

"It's not my dog" is a phrase I use to dis-
tance myself from a problem I don't want to deal
with. It's like when someone else's dog poops on
your lawn, and you have to clean it up. It's not
fair, it's not pleasant, and it's not your respon-

sibility. But you have to do it anyway because no one else will. It's not my dog is a way of saying that I'm not the one who caused the problem, but I'm the one who has to fix it.

Are these statements true? Does the fact that AI said them make them accurate? Is it up to you to fix the problem? And how do you know no one else will take care of it? If the neighbor's dog poops in your yard, you probably want to clean it up (or ask your neighbor to), but you could also let the rain wash it away. There are options.

I thought this answer couldn't be right, so I queried other AI programs and got the same reply. I had requested a paragraph about it's NOT my metaphorical dog, and each time, I received one telling me it IS my dog, whether I want it or not.

AI was drawing on the collective content for this answer, and it affirmed that people often feel responsible for cleaning up messes they did not create. While taking ownership of our actions and mistakes is essential, it's equally important to recognize that not all problems are ours to solve.

Constantly trying to fix things is an old rationale that can be exhausting and unproductive. We must prioritize what matters most to us and focus our energy on that while not getting distracted by all the shiny objects vying for our attention. We don't have time or energy for all of them.

Some inspirations come quickly and blink out just as fast, while others stay around for a lifetime. We bring the ones we are attracted to into our lives and enjoy them, but one day, they may no longer hold the fascination they once did. This is when we say, "This is no longer my dog."

My company transferred me to Cleveland, Ohio, to help open a real estate branch office. Our space was located downtown in a newly renovated building on Superior Street. I was out of my league living and working in such a large metropolis.

There were things like having to hire an attorney to get my daughter into high school, living in an apartment that a man named Petey died in and had never left, snow blowing sideways off of Lake Erie, and a salesman who told me he would not sell me a car unless I brought my husband in to discuss it.

I often recalled when the company partner asked me to go to Cleveland, and I replied, "Why not?" After being there a few days, I realized my response should have been, "Why?" But no matter, I was committed and decided to make the most of the opportunity as it would be an experience I couldn't get elsewhere, so I settled into my new surroundings.

Outside of work, I volunteered with several organizations, one of which was Hospice of the Western Reserve. It was rewarding, and I enjoyed interacting with the staff and my patients. I was with them for the three years I lived in Cleveland. I spent one year doing home care and the rest of the time in the hospital's hospice unit. I liked both, but I preferred the hospice unit.

When our office was up and running and had adequate staff, I felt I had fulfilled my obligation and was free to leave the area. I was not at all sad to head west to Boulder, Colorado, which was a well-earned break from the heaviness of

Ohio. I lived in Boulder for many years, and I gave thanks every day for sunshine, mountain vistas, beautiful weather, kind people, my editing job, and being able to work the hours I chose from my home office.

Years later, I moved to Rapid City, South Dakota. I had spare time and looked for somewhere to volunteer, and I remembered the joy I had working for the hospice in Cleveland. When Hospice of Rapid City offered training, I enrolled, thinking that might be what I was looking for. It wasn't.

The work environment and expectations differed, and I was surprised that I no longer felt drawn to do the work. I was good at it, and it had been fulfilling in the past, but I had changed over the years. It was no longer a fit for me. I was glad I recognized this early so the staff did not waste hours training me, thinking I would be part of the team.

Once a company has invested time and training in an individual, they naturally expect that person to work for them. The hospice needed volunteers, so it wasn't easy, but I had to tell them that I would not be completing the training as I had changed my mind. Doing something just because it is expected rarely benefits anyone. When we express our feelings and intentions openly and honestly, it fosters healthy and productive relationships.

Being a hospice volunteer had been my dog, but it was time to rehome it as it no longer belonged to me; it was now someone else's. I felt relieved when I decided, "This is not my dog."

The Takeaway: What was once ours may no longer be.

Story 5
Angry Dog

"When you see something beautiful in someone,
tell them. It may take a second to say,
but for them, it could last a lifetime."
THE MINDS JOURNAL

Foster homes can be a fresh start if the new parents cherish the child. Unfortunately, not all people who foster children provide a nurturing environment, especially if they go into the arrangement for selfish reasons. If they consider the benefits they will receive while overlooking the child's needs, they instead create a toxic atmosphere. Being a foster parent means caring for and supporting the youngster through thick and thin. But that is not always how it plays out.

When I was thirteen, I broke my ankle in
two places while roller skating. I had just moved
into a foster home in August of that year. When
the roller rink owner called my foster mother and

told her I had hurt my leg, she said, "Take her out and shoot her." The man was stunned and took me to the hospital instead.

I was accepted into that home because I knew how to cook, clean, and care for their five children under age six. With my leg in a cast and hobbling on crutches, I could not do all of my chores, which angered my foster mother. Not only couldn't I do my work, but she now had to drive me to and from school since walking the two miles on crutches was out of the question. She called my social worker and said, "Take her back." He persuaded her to wait.

Our school was in an old three-story building with no elevator. The flights were high and steep, each having about 30 steps. My classmates taunted me, saying I was going down the wrong way and that I should put my best foot forward instead of putting the crutches down the step first. I tried to tell them that would not work. They wouldn't believe me, so I attempted to prove it when I was halfway down the flight. I put my best foot forward and fell the rest of the way, cracking my cast and bruising my body.

I'm not sure I knew I would fall, but I did know that was not a good idea. Of course, this angered my foster mother even more since she now had to take me for X-rays and to have the cast replaced. Our relationship had not been pleasant, but the accident didn't help.

For the five years that I lived there, my foster mother was angry with me most of the time, and there was little I did that met with her approval, no matter how hard I tried to please her. Doing more than she told me only increased the demands.

It is hard for an impressionable child or teen to separate themselves from things they hear repeatedly. When children receive positive feedback, they build confidence and self-respect. But when they predominately receive criticism, they question themselves and their self-worth. It is easy to make someone else's anger our own and go through life with those dogs nipping at our heels.

When we have children, whether they are our own, adopted, or classroom students, we accept what they bring to the relationship. There may be problems we never expected, but being an angry dog is not the way to deal with them. Most everyone gets annoyed occasionally, but for some, it is their nature to be bitter and cross. If this is the case, it is better to quit teaching, get a nanny, or give the child back.

One might think that being tough on a child builds character, but there is a fine line between character-building and soul-destroying.

Building self-esteem and releasing the pain I experienced as a teen took time. I first had to recognize that my foster mother was an unhappy person and that it was her anger and lack of self-worth that caused her to use me as her scapegoat. It's sad but true that not all dogs take care of their pups.

If you've had a negative experience with an angry dog, building a positive self-image is important. You can start by recognizing and acknowledging that the person's behavior hurt you. Know that their anger and aggression are not your fault, and you can let them go because they are not yours.

We begin to heal when we can say, "That is not my dog."

The Takeaway: *We may never know how our words affect another.*

Story 6
Faithful Dog

"Wise men speak because they have something to say,
fools because they have to say something."

PLATO

Have you ever felt caught in a situation with no graceful way out, knowing things would not end well no matter how you responded?

I had just met Theresa. She worked with Mary, who rented a studio apartment attached to the home of my friend Abigail. Theresa told me that Mary had Covid and was also planning to move out of the apartment.

Abigail was terrified of getting Covid and did not know she had been exposed to it while Mary was doing laundry in her part of the house. Abigail also did not know that Mary was planning to move. Surely, she would like a heads-up to increase her self-care by resting more and boosting her supplements. She would also want to begin thinking about filling the vacated apartment.

I knew Theresa would not like it, but since Abigail had been my friend for 30 years, I felt obligated to tell her, so I did. Abigail was upset, but when we talked a few days later, she was no longer concerned. It didn't seem to matter that Mary had knowingly exposed her and had said nothing about it or that she had plans to move.

Later that week, I texted Theresa to ask if she wanted to go to a concert, and she did not reply; I have not heard from her since. Mary no doubt said something to her, and she felt she couldn't trust me, which is reasonable. At the time, I thought my friendship with Abigail demanded I say something. Would Theresa have become a good friend? Possibly. But I will never know.

After thinking about it, I realized that Abigail did not want to hear what I had to say because she was friends with Mary, and knowing that information meant she had to make a choice. Would she remain quiet, or would she say something to Mary?

She did speak to her, but Mary talked her way out of it. Would I have been a better friend if I had kept quiet and let things play out?

Would you speak up if you knew something you thought a friend would want to know? And if your friend was aware of something that affected you, would you like them to tell you? Making this decision can be difficult.

There are times when it is questionable whether we should be a faithful dog. In our confusion, we may make choices we later see were not the greatest. We do our best, but even if we make a seemingly wrong choice, we learn something. The next time, we may say, "That is not my dog."

The Takeaway: Friends may not want or need our protection.

Story 7
Rabid Dog

"Let the buyer beware!"
ENGLISH PROVERB

It is easy to take on problems that don't belong to us, but at other times, we may not own up to the things that are ours. How often do we pass the buck? If we agree to something and don't follow through, it's like leaving a dog to fend for itself. And if we're not careful, that dog could become rabid and infect those around it.

In our everyday lives, we have agreements with people and businesses. For example, when we go shopping, we expect the store's employees to help us find the product we need and give us accurate information to make an informed decision. And if we have issues with our purchase, we assume they will help resolve them.

Smaller stores would not stay in business if they didn't honor this agreement and give excellent service. Many of the big box stores, however, don't care about providing a good experience for their shoppers. Because of their sales volume, they can offer lower prices that encourage people to go there despite the poor service. Their customers know and accept this. Those unaware of the company's track record can get caught in a merry-go-round experience of whose job it is to fix the situation when things go wrong. I was one of those people.

On September 9th, I ordered an LG stackable washer and dryer from the home store. Three weeks later, on September 29th, they delivered them, but the washer had a dent in it, and the delivery man, who was wiser than me, advised me to refuse delivery. Little did I know that the store considered it a done deal once I accepted it; there was no thirty-day return policy.

Over the next two months, I made numerous calls to find out where my replacement washer was. Each time I talked to an employee, they said it would be delivered and gave me a date, but it never came. There was no reason; it just didn't come. Finally, a lady at the 800 number canceled that order and placed another.

The washer arrived on November 30th, three months after I had initially placed the order. When they put the dryer on top of it, the dryer cord was too short to reach the outlet. The delivery man told me he couldn't fix it and that I should call the store. After they left, I opened the washer, and the chemical smell almost knocked me over. Now what?

I made multiple trips to the store and was on the phone for many hours over the next month trying to resolve this. I ran load after load with detergent, bleach, baking soda, vinegar, and Affresh (a freshener to clean washers), none of which removed the smell. Finally, LG scheduled a repairman. The day he was to come, he called and told me he was canceling the order because "all washers smell," and it was not his job to install a longer cord. Back to the phone.

The 800 operators tried to transfer me to the local store manager four times. I was on hold each time for so long that it timed out. Finally, an operator sent an email to the district and store managers. The store manager answered it, passing responsibility for the washer to LG, and said it was up to me to replace the dryer cord, even though I had paid for the installation package.

The home store's management is an example of people who refuse to take responsibility. Satisfying the purchaser is their concern because they stock the products and accept the customers' money for them. It turns out that they only want to function as a warehouse. Once it goes out the door, it doesn't come back, and any issues are between the customer and the product manufacturer, even if the person bought the store's warranty.

It can be frustrating if you don't know this ahead of time. If you did know, you would save yourself the headache and shop elsewhere, or you would have no expectations.

I didn't know how to resolve this, but the store manager didn't care. Since he had the title of Manager, he was liable for every sale at that store, yet he passed responsibility to LG and me, saying it was not his problem.

Can there be a resolution when dealing with people who will not be accountable or stores that do not value their customers enough to stand behind their merchandise? Trying to get that person to be accountable can be frustrating when we are left on our own to handle it.

I considered hiring an attorney, but their fees would have cost more than new appliances. So, I did the only other thing I could think of—I turned to social media. The response was staggering, as people told stories about this company, and I regretted not asking for their advice before the purchase. When I told the store manager this, he did not seem phased. He still would not help me, although the company eventually paid to replace the dryer cord, hoping I would disappear.

I sold the washer and dryer to a couple who put them in their basement, so the smell would be no problem. I lost $400 on the deal but was glad I recovered most of my money, and, more importantly, I learned never to enter that store again.

There may be circumstances that prevent us from fulfilling our promises as initially planned. In those cases, it's up to us to renegotiate. If others do not follow through on their deals with us, we do what we can to address the situation, and if nothing changes, it is okay to conserve our energy and walk away. We should only choose battles that we feel are worth fighting. It's important to learn when to say, "That is not my dog."

The Takeaway: Be aware and pick your battles.

Story 8
Needy Dog

> *"One who believes in himself has*
> *no need to convince others."*
> LAO TZU

It is human nature to want to receive love. To many, this means being acknowledged. They will go to great lengths to get attention, positive or negative, because they associate it with being loved, never realizing these can be two different things. In the process, they alienate people who would have been their friends.

Thomas lived in my apartment complex. I met him several years ago, and we went to breakfast and emailed a few times. He stopped communicating when I disagreed with something he said. (I don't remember what it was.)

Since he lived close by, I saw him period-ically, and for a while, I waved or called out a hello. He pretended he didn't see or hear me. One day, while he was walking his cat, I approached him to say hi, and he told me he was too busy to talk. At the time, he was standing there watching the cat play. Okay, I can take a hint. After that, he sometimes walked by my apartment and stopped outside. He never came to the door; he just stood there.

I am not sure why he did that, but I sus-pect he wanted me to come out and engage with him. I had tried that, and it didn't work. I asked myself if I wanted a friend who couldn't have someone disagree with him without pouting or getting angry with me. The answer was no.

I was not interested in a friendship with someone who needed to have his ego stroked and punished me when I didn't. Like a dog with a bone, he had the toy of self-righteousness and would not drop it. Interacting or playing with a dog who won't let things go is extremely difficult. It might be possible to bring a person like this around through lots of love and patience, but is that where we want to put our time and energy? Perhaps. But in this case, I did not.

We can offer compliments and support to others, but ultimately, it's up to them to feel good about themselves. If they don't, no amount of external validation will fill that void.

People cling to things that make them feel secure, even if they don't bring them happiness or fulfillment. Whether it's the need to always be right, staying in a relationship that doesn't promote joy, or being stuck in a job that doesn't align with one's passions, it is important to examine whether these things truly bring value to one's life. Perhaps letting go of them would open new avenues for a more satisfying experience.

You may choose to participate in a relationship with such a person if you feel the benefits are worth the costs, even if it is not fulfilling. It is your life, and it is up to you if you claim a needy dog, but remember, not all people require that you stroke their egos. Some would welcome a loving friendship with you, and you deserve to be with someone who inspires joy and happiness. So, before committing to a needy relationship, ask yourself if that person is the best fit for you. It may be time to say, "This is not my dog."

The Takeaway: Getting attention does not necessarily equal being loved.

Story 9
Mean Dogs

"Handle every situation like a dog. If you can't eat it or play with it, just pee on it and walk away."
GUGGIGIRL

Some people interact with others while thinking about what that person can do for them. They are always looking at what they can get for little or nothing. Alan is the opposite. He always puts others before himself, often sacrificing his time and energy to help them. Because of this, Alan is frequently taken advantage of.

When Alan's Uncle Fred and Aunt Miriam invited him to their home on the mesa (a flat-top mountain) in southern Colorado, he decided to take the trip. He and his dog Lulu would drive to Colorado in his camper, spend a few days with them, and then meet me in the Black Hills in South Dakota.

Since Alan is genuinely gifted and can fix anything, Uncle Fred saw this as an excellent opportunity and had an extensive list of things that needed building or repair. Surely, Alan would want to spend his vacation doing this work!

Aunt Miriam was housesitting off the mesa and wanted Alan to come there before accompanying Fred to their home. Since I was traveling through that area, I joined them for dinner. The twenty-mile bumpy gravel road to the house where Miriam was housesitting was dreadful, but I knew from experience that the rutted, muddy trail to their place on the mesa would be even worse. I wondered how Alan's camper would handle it.

I told Alan to consider leaving his truck there and riding with Fred since there were many more miles of bad gravel and then mud. I tried to describe it to Alan, but Fred and Miriam pushed my words aside and assured him it wasn't that bad.

They told him this because Miriam didn't want Alan to take Lulu to her house unless he had the camper for the dog to stay in, and Fred needed a worker bee. I listened as they said whatever was necessary, including outright lying. Auntie and Uncle convinced him that driving his camper to their house would be no problem. I shrugged as there was nothing more to say.

The trip went as I expected. Alan let Miriam think everything was okay but told me it was a nightmare. His vehicle shook until things flew off the shelves, eggs broke, and mustard exploded. The dog cowered in fear. When he got to their house, he spent his days checking things off Fred's to-do list. Helping with some things would have been okay, but Fred worked him from sunup to sundown. It was all work and no play; this was not a vacation.

Once Alan left Colorado, he was to drive to Custer State Park in South Dakota, where we had reserved a vendor booth at the Buffalo Roundup. He had brought live-edge wood slabs to sell, and I had my artwork. He called me and said his truck had broken down in Colorado and again in Wyoming. The engine had been jostled so severely on the bumpy roads that it had *damaged parts. Despite being in no man's land, he got what he needed and fixed it. As I said, he can repair anything, but this made him a day late, and he arrived in a bad mood.*

I was upset at how they had treated him and that it had interfered with our plans to sight-see before the Roundup, so I spoke up. When I texted Miriam, she said, "I'm taking no responsibility for it. Alan's the one that made the decision. And if his truck was in that bad shape, he shouldn't have brought it; he should have flown." She never acknowledged that he had based his decision on what they told him. They also did not pay him for the work he did. He was kin, and it was expected.

Miriam accepted no responsibility in this interaction. In his naivety, Alan got left with a mean dog and the bites it gave him. What did Alan gain from this? I can't say, but I also took on a dog. It may not have been mine when it began, but it became mine when it interfered with our plans, and I spoke up. Miriam didn't care about that either. She said, "You'll just have to do things another time."

This situation helped me reaffirm that mean and selfish people have no place in my world. Shortly after this experience, hurtful people magically faded from my life. Alan told me he did not confront Miriam and Fred because he didn't want them to feel bad.

Having unkind people in our lives is painful, but many of us do not realize we have a choice and can say no. Instead, we chalk it up to experience and go on with our day. Hopefully, without having too many experiences like this, we learn to say, "That is not my dog."

The Takeaway: Mean dogs refuse to see their part in what happens.

Story 10
Barking Dogs

"When you are immune to the opinions and actions of others, you won't be a victim of needless suffering."
Don Miguel Ruiz

Growing up, I remember being on the receiving end of hurtful comments. It wasn't easy, but I always tried not to let those words affect me. I used to tell myself, "Sticks and stones may break my bones, but words will never hurt me." Looking back, I'm not sure I believed that, but it helped me manage some tough times.

It would be wonderful if we lived in a world where people never said hateful things and we felt loved enough to reject any negativity that did come our way. Unfortunately, the reality is that many struggle with low self-esteem and self-doubt, which can make us vulnerable to accepting hurtful words as if they were true. It's important to remember that the opinions of others do not determine our worth. It is also good to surround ourselves with positive, uplifting people who support and encourage us.

The words we repeatedly hear are powerful in shaping our reality and influencing our internal dialogue. If our self-talk becomes negative, it can be more damaging than hurtful external words. Imagine the possibilities if we took control of our thoughts and used their strength to transform our self-image. By mastering our inner dialogue, we can shape a more positive future for ourselves.

Since I grew up hearing unkind words, I learned to consider what was said before I accepted it. I saw that the words people spoke could only hurt me if I believed them, and often, these folks had no idea what they were talking about. Such was the case with Jane.

Jane was someone I had known for a few years. We didn't see each other often, and I was happy that she came for a visit. After a week, I was relieved when she left. Her frenetic energy, with its many ups and downs, was exhausting.

She was right about everything, and you would never change her mind about anything.

At dinner the night before she left, she told me how much she loved me and looked up to me. Then, she began pointing out a list of things that were wrong with me. At first, I wondered who she was talking about and then realized it was me! She ended that part of the conversation by telling me to think about what she said. For a minute, I did and realized what she was saying was based on how she sees the world; this was not about me. I was not accepting it.

Why would someone fire off everything wrong with you after saying they loved and looked up to you? Is that love? They say they are telling you these things for your own good, but how do they know what is good for you? Even if you see what they say is true, it doesn't matter because their opinions do not define you. What they see as a flaw could actually be your greatest strength.

They think they must save you from yourself, but no one needs saving. Life is a smorgasbord of experiences, and we get to choose which ones we want, knowing that we also get to deal with the consequences. If we accept what others say, it becomes ours, along with the energy tossed at us when they say it. Someone else's opinion is only ours to the extent we allow it. The one that Jane wanted me to accept was definitely not mine!

After pointing out my flaws, she suddenly changed and called me her teacher and guru. She claimed I was her inspiration and asked me not to make her take me off the pedestal she had me on. She meant this as a compliment, but I told her to take me off because it was not me but her own inner strength that had helped her overcome her struggles. The last thing I wanted was to be a guru and responsible for another's actions. That was no more mine than the one she had tried to give me earlier!

When we accept credit for things that go right for others, we must also accept blame if they don't. I chose not to take either; they did not belong to me. Ultimately, we are responsible for our circumstances and must accept the consequences of our choices. We can't credit or blame anyone; it is our own doing.

If we find ourselves surrounded by individuals who cause drama and negativity, removing ourselves from those situations and seeking out more positive influences is okay. Life is too short to be surrounded by negative energy.

It is up to us to choose the people we interact with and what we want from those relationships. If we desire happiness, that means saying no to toxic people. It's not always easy, but it's the right thing to do for our well-being. Goodbye, barking dogs!

The Takeaway: Just because someone says something doesn't mean we must accept it.

Story 11
Stray Dog

*"No matter what obstacles come their way,
street pups have no problem pushing forward."*

UNKNOWN

Stray dogs roam the streets. Perhaps they want a handout or someone to give them a home. Some are just wandering around, while others are lost. In their confusion, they can create situations others have to deal with. How do you respond when encountering a stray dog?

I stopped at the light on Alta Vista and St. Francis. As I waited for the light to change, I felt a jolt. The car behind me had struck my car. I got out to see the damage and asked the guy who was still in his car to back up so I could see the bumper.

He made no attempt to move his car, so I went to his window and again asked him to back up. Instead, he slowly and painstakingly got out

48

of his old white Chevy and shuffled to the front of it. He said, "It isn't that bad. Our cars kissed." I replied, "Cars don't kiss; you hit mine!" And again, repeated, "Back up." We were blocking traffic, and I wanted to see the damage and know whether to call the police.

He didn't move but rambled on about a car that took his door off in a parking lot. I told him, "Your door is open now, and cars are whizzing around the corner. That could happen again." He paid no heed.

This situation was getting weirder by the minute, and I again instructed him to back up. He continued talking and refused to move. The light changed, and the car ahead of me drove away, so I said, "Okay, I will pull forward." I moved my car and returned to survey the situation. As I was looking at the bumper, his vehicle came forward and hit mine again! He had failed to put it in Park when he got out, and it coasted ahead on its own.

The damage was minor, so I told him to forget it. I got in my car and pulled closer to the *intersection. The light changed, and as I drove off, I saw him walking up to another vehicle with a pen and paper, presumably to copy down its license plate number. Little did he know that was not the car he had struck.*

He was a stray dog that was more than I could handle. If he had been a four-legged dog, I would have called the owner or the animal shelter to come and get him. But what do you do with a two-legged stray that won't listen? I did not know how to help him since he seemed oblivious to all I said. He had caused minor damage to my vehicle, so I did not need to file a report; there was nothing more for me to do. Did he need help? Perhaps. But he was not my dog.

The Takeaway: Getting hit once is not fun; getting hit twice within ten minutes is just plain crazy!

Story 12
Good Dog

"If standing up for yourself burns a bridge,
I have matches. We ride at dawn."

UNKNOWN

Family can be our greatest blessing, and it can also pose significant challenges, sometimes both. These relationships are often the most complicated ones in our lives. There can be many kinds of characters in a family—kind, loving, lying, helpful, selfless, troublemakers, cheaters, and bullies, to name a few.

Considering my three families, I have had five parents. I am the second oldest of fifteen brothers and sisters—three biological, six half, and six foster, so I have had many parental and sibling relationships.

My birth mother was a loving, devoted parent; she died when I was five. My father remarried, and his new wife was mentally ill and abusive; some called her wicked. At thirteen, I went to live in a foster home. My foster father and I had great talks and laughed a lot. He taught me things like how to drive, change oil, and replace a tire. He died young. His wife was not so kind; she only accepted me into their home because she needed someone to cook, clean, and care for the five children. She rarely spoke to me except to tell me what to do or complain about something I had done. Her favorite line was, "You're grounded!"

My older biological sister and I love each other despite being very different. We live many miles apart but periodically come together to share what we have in common, like our love of ice cream. My blood brother was a kind-hearted man I loved very much; he died young. My younger sister and I have had no contact for years.

The six half-siblings were not part of my life once I entered the foster home. I did try to maintain a relationship with two of them, but they followed their mother's lead and were not nice people.

For 64 years, I believed that my foster siblings were my family. However, it turned out that only two of them considered me their sister. Despite my efforts, I was never part of that family. I loved them, but apparently, they did not feel the same way. I don't know why.

We want our family's love. To get their approval, we try to meet their expectations, but doing so is not always possible. It can be complicated when they do things like schedule events and expect everyone to attend, no matter the cost or inconvenience. Such was the case with my foster mother's 90th birthday.

Hortensia's 90th birthday was approaching, and to help her celebrate, her sister organized a luncheon at her exclusive retirement community. Hortensia always expected her children to participate in her parties so she could count how many were present and then proudly tell her friends, "All of my children came." It wasn't that she wanted to visit with all of us, but it was a matter of how many showed up. Rarely was I considered one of the children, but in the counting game, I was.

53

Her party was held in the summer of 2020, during the height of Covid. The rule for attending this birthday function was to be vaccinated and have had at least one booster. For health reasons, I chose not to get vaccinated. But the rules were the rules, and the family told me that if I came to the party, I would have to wear both a mask and a face shield, which presented a problem since this was a luncheon. The other rule was social distancing. These requirements meant I would be seated in a corner with my mask and shield, unable to eat or visit with anyone. Really? Yet I was expected to be there?

Over the years, I had tried to please Hortensia, but nothing ever satisfied her. A few years before this party, I realized there was no point in going to extremes to do what she expected because her attitude toward me was not going to change. But this was her 90th! I wanted to help her celebrate this milestone, but I could not meet the requirements.

The expectation that I attend the party despite the obstacles helped me make the final decision that I could stop working so hard to be the good dog. Being part of the headcount was no longer mine either. I was free to say, "These are not my dogs."

The Takeaway: You can't please everyone.

Story 13
Happy Dog

*"When I feel inadequate, unloved, and unworthy, I
remember who I am and straighten my crown."*

UNKNOWN

Making people happy can be fun, but it can
also have a downside. We may have developed this
tactic as children to get attention or protect ourselves. If we made adults smile, they rewarded us
with special treats, or perhaps it kept us from getting punished.

The drawback of doing things to please others is their happiness will be temporary. Since it
does not come from within them, they continually
rely on outside stimuli to provide experiences that
generate that feeling. Trying to keep someone
happy can quickly become a burden.

Although joy and happiness are often used
interchangeably, there is an important difference
between the two. Happiness is usually a fleeting

emotion triggered by external circumstances, such as receiving good news or achieving a goal. Joy, on the other hand, is a profound and more sustainable feeling that comes from within and is not dependent on external factors. It is a state of "being" characterized by peace and inspiration. While happiness brings temporary satisfaction, joy lasts and brightens even the darkest days.

Our animal friends find happiness in simple pleasures like going for walks, being petted, having regular meals, and getting a treat now and then. For humans, it is more complex. While gifts and accomplishments can bring momentary gratification, they may not be satisfying in the long term unless the feeling comes from inside first.

It is easy to forget to look within when we are caught up in the daily hustle and bustle of life, but if we relax and breathe when we are feeling down or going through tough times, we will more likely find joy and answers.

Something we can do to help ourselves bring joy forward is to sing a song like *Put on a Happy Face* from the 1960s movie "Bye-Bye Birdie;" it can lift our mood and stimulate joy. Once in that space, we can maintain it by feeling gratitude for our lives, the beauty around us, the people who love and care for us, and our many experiences.

If we have difficulty doing this, one option is to seek help from professionals, but they, too, may struggle to find their inner joy.

Grace is a psychotherapist. When I met her, she had a pleasant smile and a calm exterior, but I felt sadness underneath that. As she talked, it became clear that she loved her work, but it was taking its toll. She felt her patients' pain and had taken it on as her own. Throughout the day, she wore a gentle, reassuring smile so her clients would feel safe confiding in her, but that was not how she felt. Her patients spoke highly of her and got the relief they wanted. However, if Grace was to continue her work, she needed to learn that being there for them was her job, but carrying the load for them was not.

Outer things can help us feel good, but no one can provide joy for us, and we can't give it to others. Nonetheless, we can contribute to the sense of positivity that someone already has, and they can do the same for us.

Whatever we feel, it is essential to remain true to ourselves and not try to be something we aren't; embracing our emotions and being genuine are necessary for meaningful relationships. If we have been using a happy face to hide behind, letting that false facade go can be liberating. However, at the same time, we never want to underestimate the impact a smile can have on bringing about the positive energy we seek.

To live authentically and leave that false happy dog behind, it's time to say, "That is not my dog!"

The Takeaway: Pretending happy is out; being authentic is in.

Story 14
Free-Range Dog

"Your life should be wonderful."
SARA EYESTONE

It was 20 degrees and lightly snowing. As I drove down St. Francis Drive, I saw people huddled in coats and blankets, standing on corners, waiting for someone to hand them money. Some didn't bother holding the typical rectangular cardboard with illegible writing saying something about every bit helps, God bless you, or Viet Nam vet; everyone knows why they are there, and if one chooses to give, they hand them a bill. On this day, I saw something new: a bucket hanging on a pole, and no one was there. That was one way to avoid the cold!

No matter the weather, people are always panhandling at busy intersections or outside stores. They often stand under a street sign that says, "Avoid panhandlers. Give to local charities," or next to a building placard that reads, "No loitering." Recently, the city installed a new sign on corners that reads, "If you need food or shelter, call 212."

One day, I was in my car waiting for the sales clerk to print my photos. I watched as person after person came out of the store and handed the man standing under the "No Loitering" sign a bill—I don't know the denomination.

No words were spoken. The man was nicely dressed and had no sign asking for money; he may have just been standing there. He took in a substantial amount of cash, so if he was panhandling, there was little motivation to change his situation. And if he wasn't, perhaps it was time to start.

Santa Fe, New Mexico, has resources to help those experiencing homelessness and prefers they get help through the designated centers instead of receiving it on the street. This way, they have their needs met while minimizing less helpful purchases.

So, why do people give to individuals rather than donate to local resource houses? It could be a moment of compassion or guilt for having more than someone else. It could be programming from their upbringing or an impulsive act while waiting at the stoplight. Or perhaps it is distrust in organizations to distribute funds effectively. Everyone has their motivations.

While it is true that there are organizations where the intended recipients see very little of the funds, there are also reputable centers that provide meals, clothing, shelter, and other needed items. When I visited one, I was impressed by the people who worked there; they were dedicated and hard-working.

Some panhandlers provide a unique service. When the weather is nice, one man walks back and forth at the corner with a bucket and squeegee, offering to wash windshields. A talented musician sets up his boombox in the Albertsons parking lot and plays the violin. I couldn't help but wonder if his parents saw him using his skill this way when he was a child taking lessons. There's also someone who sells newspapers and a trio of musicians who play guitar and tambourine and sing in the parking lot by Trader Joe's. All of these people brighten the day for passersby. I often find myself stopping and listening to their music, and it makes me smile. Giving them a few bucks to show my appreciation is a joy.

The number of panhandlers is growing. They all have their reasons, and it may be necessary for some. However, there are individuals like the one my friend spoke with. She asked her why she didn't get a job. The lady replied, "I get three meals a day at the center; they give me a place to sleep, and the money I get on the corner is my spending money. Why would I work?"

Another lady in her new car approached me in the Sprouts grocery store parking lot and asked for $10. She had my attention! After we talked, I asked her why she was driving around asking for money, and she said it was her "lifestyle." She couldn't tell me what that meant, but she knew it involved getting money from strangers.

Besides the trash they leave behind, these folks usually do not cause trouble or damage property. There are some, however, that do create problems. The following is a post that appeared on our local news board.

The property behind us was purchased last year, and the new owners did some demolition and cleanup, and it is now a vacant lot. In the last six months, the homeless have set up camp on this lot, and they have done significant damage to our property. They have cut the chain link fence and barbed wire multiple times, broken into our shed, and stolen items. Today our morning was spent cleaning the yard from their overnight stay—removing blankets, clothes, trash, cigarette butts, human waste, and drug paraphernalia.

We're sad and angry that we have to repair the fence again. The police won't come, and our insurance company won't let us file any more claims for the damage. We have not been able to locate the property owner about the squatters. No matter how you feel about trespassers, we should have a common goal: finding a solution for our homeless. Is there a solution?

Several people responded to this post. One suggested going together with neighbors and hiring a security company. Others mentioned getting a mean dog, installing a motion-sensor sprinkler system, and adding bright lights.

I included this notice because you may have a similar situation that is draining your energy. The lady who posted it asked if there was a solution, which is a good question. Let's consider that.

A friend who returned from Scottsdale, Arizona, said that city had clean streets, no graffiti, and no street people. To deal with homelessness, the residents pay a yearly $50 tax that is used to buy abandoned buildings that are turned into apartments for them; panhandling is against the law. The first time the police arrest a person asking for money, they take them to one of these shelters and give them a home. There are different facilities for singles, families, and those with mental challenges. If arrested a second time, the person goes to jail.

Rapid City, South Dakota, has a project called Giving Meters. In the downtown area, they installed green poles that look like parking meters. People can insert cash or credit cards to contribute to homeless projects.

In Eugene, Oregon, there are so many people on the streets that the city officials want to relocate them to the coastal towns. Of course, there is already no shortage of homeless on the coast.

Homelessness is a complex issue that requires innovative solutions. It's encouraging to see cities experimenting with different approaches to tackle the problem, but we have a long way to go. It's essential for policymakers and think tanks to collaborate and find practical solutions to address this growing situation.

In the meantime, we can examine what our responsibility is. Do we pray, send money, offer our services, blame God and the government, or say, "Wow! That's too bad; I'm glad that's not happening to me?"

We can have many reactions when we encounter someone asking for help, and it is up to us whether we offer our support and to whom. If we choose to donate, it's best to give with joy and respect. Only then will our contribution truly be a gift.

Offering solutions or a helping hand can be a rewarding experience and a way to give to your community. If you have the means and the desire to help, do so. But you may also choose to say, "That is not my dog."

The Takeaway: The greatest gift we can offer anyone is respect.

Story 15
Compassionate Dog

"It takes courage to grow up and become who you really are."

E.E. CUMMINGS

It is a misguided belief that we have a responsibility to take on the problems of others, and often those of the world. I suspect this comes from the age-old mindset, "He ain't heavy—he's my brother."

We are told to have compassion for others. According to online dictionaries, "compassion" means " suffering with." They also say the word implies "pity and an urgent need to fix the problem."

I do not accept this idea, as no one should suffer; if someone chooses that, and usually it is a choice, why would we want to join them? How can we help if we are with them in their sinking boat? Instead, we must stay in a solid place to offer a hand when they are ready.

Although it is considered brotherly love to take on someone's problems as our own, it is not love; it is enabling. We may feel pressure to be the superhero who saves the day, but it's essential to ask ourselves if our involvement would prevent the other person from developing their own superpowers.

William had tough times off and on for years with alcohol, trouble at home, and holding a job. He was like a son to me, and it was hard to stand back and watch him as he wrestled with his life. After a few attempts to help, I saw getting involved was not helping. He needed to get through the tough times in his own way, and once he did, he would be wiser, more mature, and never have to go through them again. There was nothing wrong with William; he was building wisdom by experiencing the many sides of life.

Intervening in a situation can hinder a person's growth and maturity. By treating someone as helpless, we inadvertently encourage them to adopt a victim mentality. They believe they can't change their lives, so they wait for someone to rescue them when things go awry.

Balancing support with allowing individuals to learn from their mistakes empowers them to take responsibility for their actions. They develop the confidence and skills to tackle challenges and overcome obstacles, making them more resilient and self-reliant in the long run. As a result, they become more independent and able to take charge of their lives.

Until a person is ready to change, they are not open and will list many reasons why they can't alter things, and they will tell you why your ideas and suggestions won't work. Or, they agree with you and then do nothing. People only hear when they are ready, so you might as well save your breath.

It may be difficult not to interfere, but usually, you can't fix things anyway. When they have maxed out that experience and are ready to do their part to change their circumstances, then you can offer your resources. Letting them navigate their lives themselves does not mean that you abandon them; it is simply stepping back so they can step up. It's okay to say no, even if it feels difficult. Likewise, if someone tells us no, that is okay too.

Another instance when it is wise to stand down is when the person does not want our involvement. Perhaps they asked for it and then changed their mind. That decision must be honored.

I had an appointment at 3:00 p.m. to do Reiki for my friend Astrid, who was having abdominal pain. She called about noon and said her daughter was taking her to the hospital. I phoned the house later, and there was no answer, so I suspected they had kept her.

The next day, I went to the hospital, and Astrid was there but was not in her room—she was down for tests. I waited an hour and then left. When I called a family member, he said Astrid did not want to see anyone. Although she had asked me for help, things had changed. Astrid was following the course she felt was right for her. She had rehomed the dog and no longer needed me to take ownership of it.

Frequently, the most compassionate thing we can do is to allow someone to have their experience while encouraging them and letting them know we are there. We don't have to figure anything out for them; they will do that in their own time.

In the past, we believed the best way to help others was to focus on their needs and put ours on hold. It is time to stop that and start caring for ourselves, even if the idea goes against our upbringing. Resting, getting bodywork, doing things we enjoy, taking time alone, eating healthy foods, and avoiding needy people are a few things we can do. Taking care of ourselves is not selfish; rather, it is necessary so we have the energy to help others when required. As they say, put your oxygen mask on first.

One caution I will add here is to be wary of those trying to pull you into their drama by saying they want your opinion. It makes us feel important when asked what we think, but most who start the discussion with this statement do not accept input and rarely wait for an answer before they are off on another tangent. They dump their problems and take your energy. Then you walk away feeling depleted, and they go on to the next person.

The best thing we can offer anyone is empowering them to develop their superpowers so that they become the heroes of their stories. For everyone's sake, it is best to recognize what is ours and when it is appropriate to say, "That is not my dog."

The Takeaway: Everyone can be their own superhero.

Story 16
No Boundaries Dog

"You are not a victim of anyone or anything."
21 SHAUMBRA REALIZATIONS
BY GEOFFREY HOPPE

What starts as a fun venture can quickly turn sour if those involved do not establish boundaries. It is like getting a puppy; if you don't train it immediately, you will have issues with its behavior. You teach it not to bite or bark incessantly, to potty outdoors, to stay in the yard, and that feeding times are at 7:00 a.m. and 4:00 p.m. The puppy learns and responds appropriately if the trainer stays consistent with the rules. Like dogs, people also do better when they know the parameters.

Jan had a house on a large property with an RV space. Her friend Carrie moved to town and was looking for a home to buy. While she searched, Jan allowed her to park her trailer on the land and hook up to the electric, sewer, and water. She was excited to have Carrie close by and made no provisions for rent, utilities, or how long this arrangement would last.

Jan invited her to dinner several times, and Carrie started coming every night. After dinner, she spent the evening with Jan and her family. When Jan went out for dinner, Carrie tagged along but never picked up the tab.

The house search continued, and even after purchasing one, Carrie did not move into it. This situation went on for six months, and Jan grew more unhappy. She did enjoy Carrie's company and didn't want to ruin their friendship, so she remained quiet while growing increasingly irritated.

They could have avoided hard feelings if they had made agreements at the onset or discussed the situation when it got to be too much. Since they didn't, Jan wondered how Carrie could feel this was a fair exchange. Carrie didn't know that Jan would have liked her to contribute to meals and let her and her family have some evenings to themselves. They were on two different pages, and having a conversation to let each other know how they felt could have made their time together more reciprocal.

When frustrated or angry, it's easy to misinterpret what someone says or does and build a story about them and their motives. We can avoid these misunderstandings through open and honest communication. Remembering that we all have unique perspectives and experiences and listening to and understanding each other can go a long way in fostering well-balanced relationships. It also helps to find common ground and focus on areas of agreement rather than differences.

Setting boundaries can be tricky, but determining what works and what does not is a form of self-care. Once you know your limits, you can select the parameters for the interaction. After all, your time and energy are precious, and it is up to you to use them wisely.

By speaking up, we empower ourselves to let go of the drama. When outside of it, we can see the bigger picture and focus on what truly matters. Choosing a peaceful lifestyle helps us invite kind, positive people and experiences into our lives while steering clear of the chaos. Living in a harmonious environment supports everyone's well-being.

When we want someone to be a friend, it is easy to ignore warning signs and hope things will go smoothly. Even when we do negotiate, we may agree to something we don't like because it's easier to say yes than to argue, but talking things through helps avoid stumbling blocks. This isn't rebelling, looking for pity, or seeking revenge; it expresses what is right for us. It's okay to prioritize our needs and wants, even if it means going against the expectations of others.

Ultimately, we control our lives and should make decisions that align with our values and goals. When everyone knows the boundaries, unpleasant surprises are less likely. Perhaps Jan would have been happier if she had said, "This is not my dog."

The Takeaway: Negotiate and then renegotiate.

Story 17
Pain Dog

"Kindness is the language which the
deaf can hear, and the blind can see."
MARK TWAIN

People and events come and go in our lives.
Some experiences cause us to feel happy, while
others trigger sadness. Many instances fall somewhere in between these two emotional states. One
of the most challenging situations is losing a loved
one.

Jordan's husband had cancer, and she lov-
ingly cared for him as he had for her all the years
that they were together. When Bill died, Jordan's
life turned upside down. Her companion and the
love of her life were no longer there. Her life had
centered around him. What did she have left?

Jordan and Bill had been my friends for
sixty years, but we rarely got together after I
married and moved away. Bill's passing opened

an opportunity for Jordan and me to reconnect and allowed me to share this time of transition with her.

When someone we care about is struggling, it can be challenging to know how to help. In an effort to comfort them, we may take on the person's pain and suffer with them, but that doesn't accomplish much. Telling them to put on their big-girl boots and get on with life or sharing our own stories of suffering may not be helpful either. Disappearing from their lives can add more pain to what they already have. Usually, it's best to listen with no agenda other than to be present for them. Letting them know we care can be a powerful way to provide support.

Managing grief is a personal experience and different for everyone, but sharing that experience can bring people closer even if they don't know each other well. Feeling comfortable enough to share their emotions with you can be a gift for someone struggling with loss.

As you listen, know they may feel this way today and differently tomorrow—our feelings are transitory. Also, remember that it is not your responsibility if a person gets stuck in their sorrow, nor is it your accomplishment when they move past it. They do it themselves. You can be there, but ultimately, how they feel is up to them.

Now, back to Jordan's story.

Jordan felt broken. Her daughter suggested she move to her area, which Jordan did after allowing herself time to grieve by visiting the gravesite every day, sorting through Bill's things, and crying while sitting in his chair. She began looking forward to being close to family and getting to know her daughter as an adult; she would build a new life.

Within a short time after her move, she made friends, spent time with her grandson, created a garden, and joined a church; her days began to fly by. She said she still felt the loss but was healing as she made a life in her new home.

When we go through a traumatic event, it is natural to feel overwhelmed. We want to acknowledge and embrace those emotions, but we don't want to get stuck in them. By allowing ourselves to feel whatever comes up, we can better know what steps to take to heal. This will differ for everyone, so we must find what works for us, but perhaps being in nature or writing will help.

Doctors sometimes prescribe medication to help people cope with trauma. Drugs can be a bridge to healing but can also become a crutch a person depends on. Whether one uses drugs or not, the emotions must be recognized and released to move forward and prevent unhealthy patterns from forming.

No matter how you handle your pain, be gentle with yourself during these times. It is okay not to have all the answers immediately. Sometimes, all we can do is trust and take one step at a time.

The same is true if you are helping someone else navigate their sorrow. They may not know how to move forward, but they can find their solutions, and in time, they will. It's not up to you to work things out for them. Often, they just need someone to be there with a reassuring word. Appreciate their process as they work through their emotions by respecting their pain dogs but know when to say, "This is not my dog."

The Takeaway: Acknowledging a person is the greatest gift we can give. It says, "I see you."

Story 18
Time Dogs

"The present is the only time we have."

UNKNOWN

We think that time is solid and that there are only a certain number of hours in a day and so many days in a year. This belief has made us slaves to our watches, but time is more fluid than that.

Have you ever left the house late for an appointment and arrived early? Or did you leave in plenty of time and arrive late? You look back and ask why. It was not due to traffic, as that was normal. You notice but blow it off, saying, "That was weird." Time IS weird; it can expand or contract, and we never give its fluidity credence because it seems impossible.

It can feel like time is an enemy always working against us, and constantly fighting against the clock can be overwhelming. However, it's important to remember that time can also be a valuable ally if we learn to harness its power. To do this, begin by asking yourself three questions:

- Do I accept responsibilities that aren't mine?
- Do I clutter my life with drama and chaos?
- Do I set impossible deadlines?

If you relate to these things, examine your habits and thought patterns. You may be operating under old beliefs or expectations that no longer serve you. Why do you say yes to some things and no to others? Change starts with awareness.

Time has not been an issue for me, and I was surprised to learn that it is for many. As I listened to people breathlessly talk about how much there is to do, I felt the stress they put on themselves. It made me realize time's important role in our daily well-being.

Being mindful of what we accept is a never-ending task because it constantly changes. Challenges continually pop up, giving us opportunities to choose which responsibilities are right for us and which are not. If you want to whittle down your list, here are five things you can try:

- Screen your calls.

- Think before you commit.
- Speak up.
- Do things as they arise so you don't have to think about them again.
- Put away your to-do list for one week.

Yes, that's right! Dispense with the lists for one week. While checking a thing off is satisfying, there are usually five more that replace it, and you never seem to get ahead. The pressure of getting through the items can be overwhelming, so you don't look at your calendar but instead do other things like checking social media. Of course, this doesn't mean lists are wrong; they serve a purpose. Once you've had a break, you can return to using them with a fresh perspective.

When you make a list, schedule time for yourself and the things you enjoy, like sports, visiting friends, reading, or hiking. It is also good to leave space in your day for those unexpected things that come up. Stop the excessive planning so you can be at ease with time, making life more productive and fun.

I may not have an issue with time, but I sometimes feel life's pressures, like what insurance company I should go with, what tires are best for my car, or whether I travel now or later. When I get into worry mode, I hear Bob Newhart in my head shouting, "Stop it!" How many times have I needed that reminder? Probably more than I care to count.

Note: *"Stop it!" is a skit that Bob Newhart performed on his show many years ago, possibly in the 70s or 80s. You may find it on YouTube.*

We are all learning. We may get it tomorrow or later, but we must do things our way to have the desired experience. We often choose the hard way and only later see the valuable wisdom we gained from walking the difficult path. It has to be that way so that at the end of the day, we can say, "I did it my way and learned that was not my dog!"

The Takeaway: Time is fluid; experiment with it.

Story 19
Sit! Stay! Dog

*"Think for yourself, or others will think
for you without thinking of you."*
HENRY DAVID THOREAU

People are more than willing to tell us what to do, how we should do it, what we need, and how to feel. Commercials are one of the first things that come to mind. The companies have a product to sell, and the ad's job is to convince us that we have a problem their item will solve.

When I turn on my tablet, an ad immediately comes up. It could be for a movie, pet food, or, scariest of all, something I had Googled earlier that day. Pop-ups are everywhere online as people attempt to monetize their websites. Advertisers know that even if we don't consciously see them, they can still impact us.

Commercials are nothing new. I remember when I was a child, there were the daily soap operas my grandmother listened to on the radio and later watched on television. These shows were a means for companies to get their products in front of homemakers who cleaned the house, did the laundry, and bathed the children. They offered a different soap for every chore: Ivory soap for cleansing gentle skin, Spic and Span for scrubbing the floor, 20 Mule-Team Borax for laundry, and Bon-Ami for cleaning sinks and fixtures. This is why these programs were called soaps—they sold soap.

Television advertising was so successful that the time allotted for commercials increased from five to fifteen minutes out of every hour. The products also expanded to include streaming services, solar panels, furniture, automobiles, hygiene products, and, don't forget, pizza.

In 2020, pharmaceuticals made up 75% of television ads. They are not advertised to raise awareness but to get consumers to initiate a conversation with their doctor. But have you ever wondered how informed your physicians are about all the new drugs on the market? They may have only heard of the medication by seeing the same commercial you saw. With so many new medicines being released, it's almost impossible for them to stay current. Pharmacists may be the ones to talk with as they are more likely to know the latest compounds.

It's good to listen to what medical professionals say about our bodies and health, but it's also a good idea to do our own research before taking action. Understanding our condition can help us ask the right questions and voice our concerns. Sometimes, those discussions can lead to a new and less drastic treatment. It's all about everyone being informed to find the best solution.

Another situation of Sit! Stay! that you may encounter is while working on a project. It's common to receive advice from others, and while some suggestions may be helpful, it's good to remember that things are constantly changing, and what worked for someone else may not work for you. If you've done your research and found a better way to proceed, it's okay to decline their advice and move forward with your approach. Trust your abilities and do what's best for the project.

These are examples of the Sit! Stay! directives we receive from others, but what about the commands we give? The first one will annoy many of you, and you may disagree, and that is okay because we don't have to agree on anything. As with all scenarios described herein, they are for discussion purposes only, and everyone is free to reach their conclusions.

In times of need, many people turn to prayer. They ask a higher power to fix things they are unhappy with, like their health, finances, or relationships. Often, this pleading, bargaining, or commanding appears as if they are ordering at a fast-food restaurant.

If you are drawn to prayer, there is a way to use it more effectively. Consider asking for whatever is in the highest good. The outcome may not always align with your expectations, but it will always be for the best. Another option is to pray for healing in your heart, which will give you the strength to weather any storm with grace and clarity.

Even though we have well-meaning intentions, we often don't know what's best for ourselves or others because we don't see the bigger picture. In those moments, stepping back and letting things unfold naturally may be prudent. Surprising gifts can emerge from the experience when we trust the process. It is a wise person who knows when to let go and allow.

There are other times throughout the day when we use the Sit! Stay! command without even thinking about it. Whether typing on a keyboard or using verbal commands, we rely on our phones and computers to do everything from making phone calls, ordering food, finding entertainment, and editing photos.

As technology progresses, artificial intelligence (AI) will undoubtedly become more prevalent in our lives. While it takes on many tasks we have had to do, remember that we still have control over our decisions. Just because AI confidently presents information to us doesn't necessarily mean it is accurate. Anyone who has used GPS well knows that it is not always reliable.

It is up to us to carefully evaluate information and decide what is true and what isn't. Let's ensure we don't simply Sit or Stay when told to, but that we think critically and use discernment in all areas of our lives. Before accepting anything, ask yourself, "Is this my dog?"

The Takeaway: Think of commands as suggestions.

Story 20
Inconsiderate Dog

"Five types of people you want to surround yourself with: the inspired, the passionate, the motivated, the grateful, and the open-minded."

UNKNOWN

As I have worked to understand my responsibilities, it has gotten easier to stay true to myself. The one thing that took me longer was other people ignoring theirs. I grew up in a time when it was clear what jobs belonged to whom. Women took charge of the house and children, and men went to work. The elderly folks were respected and cared for. It was all pretty straightforward.

For better or worse, that has all changed. Now, we can create any life we want. We don't have to do what our culture previously said we should. We may not go to college, find work, have children, respect our elders, take over the family business, or follow the rules of generations gone by.

I am reminded of these differences by the teens who visit our apartment complex. They see life from a different point of view and show me that everyone has a unique perspective and experience.

I live in a senior apartment complex where grandkids often visit their grandparents. For one couple, their apartment is the kids' home away from home, and they come every day. They park as close to the building as they can, never thinking about the lady who painfully walks to her car or the man who shuffles to help his wife get from the car to their apartment. Of the six parking spaces, they usually occupy four or five.

When I told the teens, who can easily walk, that the visitor parking was across the lot, they said spaces were not assigned, so they could park where they wanted. This was true, but it did not take into account the elderly residents. It is wonderful that they spend time with their grandparents, but their choice of parking spaces creates a hardship for others.

Where they park does not directly affect me because I can walk. However, part of me was upset about this, and I questioned why. It was the disregard for those who live here that bothered me. I had spoken up, and they did not care enough about older folks to change their behavior. I decided I had to pick my battles, and this was one I was not going to win. If I wanted peace, I had to let it go and trust it would all be okay. The Serenity Prayer came to mind.

God grant me the serenity to accept the things
I cannot change, courage to change the things
I can, and wisdom to know the difference.
REINHOLD NIEBUHR

Our energy is valuable, so wasting it on things we can't change does no one any good. I told myself I would always have a parking space. I also reminded myself that expecting something from another person can lead to frustration and disappointment. Each of us has our reality, so we look at things differently, and how we navigate that reality also differs.

Throughout this book, we have discussed the importance of releasing responsibilities that are not ours. It is worth noting that some individuals refuse to accept any responsibility at all. They have a sense of entitlement and believe that they deserve special treatment and that their needs are more important than those of others.

Research has shown that this mindset can lead to feelings of isolation, disappointment, and unfulfilled expectations. How we behave and perceive ourselves is up to us, but it's important to be mindful of the potential consequences of entitlement.

The kids still park as close to the building as possible, but it stopped bothering me. However, at the time, it felt like someone thrust a puppy on me that I didn't want or ask for.

If a situation is upsetting, there is always something to gain from that experience. When you feel you have no control, look for the wisdom that is available to you from that experience. When you find it, people stop disrespecting you, the problem fades, or it will no longer bother you. You can say, "This is not my dog."

The Takeaway: Don't get your knickers in a knot.

Story 21
Lazy Dog

> *"As wonderful as dogs can be, they are famous for missing the point."*
> NATASHA SRIVASTAVA

If we love our job, we show up and give it our best effort. People who don't like their work may show up, but they get by doing as little as possible while counting the hours until they can punch out and go home.

When you're employed by someone and helping them build their business, it is easy to feel like you're just going through the motions, and there's not much reason to be fully present. But if you own the company, you have a vested interest in ensuring your customers are satisfied to keep them returning and to attract new business. This might seem obvious, but unfortunately, it's not always true.

I smelled an odd odor during the winter when I entered my single-story apartment. I couldn't identify it, yet I thought I should know what that smell was. It was too cold to open the windows, so I purchased an air filter and diffused essential oils, which helped. I was embarrassed to have anyone visit, fearing they would think I didn't properly clean my home.

A few months later, I heard noises in the attic above my living room and realized something was living up there, and the smell was from their feces! About that time, the exterminator came for his annual visit and asked if I had any activity in my apartment. I told him no bugs or rodents were inside, but something was chewing and scratching in the crawl space above my apartment. He said he would check it out.

Apparently, he didn't because the thumping, scratching, and gnawing got louder and more frequent over the next few weeks. I thought it was packrats and was concerned they would chew through the ceiling into my apartment. I told the building manager, and like the pest control man, she said she would look into it.

One day, the noise was particularly loud, and I went to her office and asked her to come and listen. When she heard them, she said, "It sounds like they are moving furniture. That is raccoons!" Indeed! It did sound like furniture was being rearranged, but I hadn't used that phrase when I talked to her because I didn't want her to think I was exaggerating. She got on the phone and called the exterminator to come back.

He was an older, heavy-set man with a vacant look in his eyes. He stood scratching his head, wondering what to do, and I said, "If I had a ladder, I would climb up to the air vent and take videos of what is in that space." He thought that was brilliant, so he got a ladder from his truck. He took videos, and we saw at least two raccoons.

He refused to climb into the crawl space to remove them; instead, he set three live traps (cages that catch the animal but don't hurt it) with marshmallows around the foundation of the building. We waited for three days, and nothing entered the traps. Meanwhile, the circus continued. I suggested he put something more tempting in the traps. Since they had dumpsters to eat from, why would they choose the marshmallows when they had to enter a confined space to get them? Disgusted with me, he got in his truck and drove away.

Finally, the apartment's maintenance man crawled into the attic and filmed three babies, but Momma was not there, so he boarded up the hole she used to enter and leave the building. He put a cage up there, and we caught the three babies that night. They were the size of cats! He took them to the animal sanctuary. I heard scratching for the next two nights as Momma tried to get back in, but eventually, she moved on.

The exterminator owned the pest control company, and despite his laziness and incompetence, he billed the complex $300 for removing three raccoons. He had not removed them—the maintenance man did the work. The complex paid him, but was it their responsibility? Perhaps.

Unfortunately, some people want the benefits without putting in the effort. The problem would disappear if we held them accountable instead of letting them get away with saying, "It's not my dog."

The Takeaway: If you have critters in your attic, get referrals before you hire an exterminator.

Story 22
Biting Dog

> *"People who say their dog doesn't bite*
> *usually have a dog that does."*
> UNKNOWN

Biting dogs come in different disguises. The most common type is a four-legged one. Another is someone who uses a harsh and biting way to avoid dealing with a situation. I have had experiences with both.

Tucker and K.C. were miniature Australian Shepherds that I pet sat throughout their lives. Even after I moved to South Dakota, I returned to Santa Fe twice a year to care for them for three weeks while their owners traveled.

One day, I was walking them along a beautiful ridge. As we were returning to the car, three golden Labs charged up the trail toward us. K.C. hid behind me, and Tucker stood watching them. The dogs ran around us, nearly knocking me over. Then one of them bit Tucker. I yelled and tried to chase him away. As the owner got close, he said not to worry as his dogs did not bite. I informed him they certainly did, as one had just bit my dog. He ignored me and casually continued down the trail. I was angry that he had blown us off.

As we approached the car, I saw that he had parked behind me. I suspected he had noticed my South Dakota license plate and decided I was not worth the bother. After we returned to the house, I checked Tucker's hip and cleaned the wound. The next day, it was worse, so I took him to the vet, who shaved the area and cleaned it.

When the couple got home, I told them what had happened. Crosley, a prominent attorney, said he knew who the dogs belonged to and would take care of it. He gave the dog's owner the vet bill, which he paid. I wished I could have seen that man's face when he found out the dog that had been bitten didn't belong to some helpless woman from South Dakota.

Another form of biting dogs is "ghosting." Ghosting refers to someone suddenly ending all communication with another without explanation and refusing to engage further. Ghosting leaves the person feeling bitten because they may have no idea what happened, and there is no opportunity for discussion.

On May 31, 2021, Bertha came to visit with all of her possessions packed on a flatbed trailer behind her SUV. She was moving from Arizona to Alabama and planned to spend a few days in Santa Fe with me on her journey east. I met her in the apartment parking lot and told her where to park, and I went inside to get my shoes.

When I came out, she had taken the trailer off the vehicle, but unbeknownst to me, she had not put chocks under the tires to stop it from rolling. I was standing there when suddenly the trailer lunged to the side, and the tongue hit the side of my left knee. I fell to the ground in what felt like slow motion. I was not in immediate pain, but I knew this was not good.

Bertha helped me get up, but I could not put weight on that leg. I had not been to a doctor since 1985, but my gut told me I needed to go to the hospital now. I hopped over to her vehicle, and she helped me get in. After packing some things that I would need, she drove me to the hospital. When we arrived, a wheelchair was sitting outside the front door. She wheeled me into the emergency room, and no one was waiting, so I went to the desk and took care of the paperwork.

They took me to a room and then wheeled my gurney down for X-rays. Bertha returned to my apartment, and I waited for the on-call doctor. When he arrived, he explained that the tibia plateau was shattered and that if I wanted to walk right, I needed surgery, but it was my choice. I called my body worker, who had patched me up after I broke my arm, to ask his thoughts, and he confirmed that, in this case, I would need surgery. So, I consented.

I had the surgery, and it was successful. I went home the next day. Bertha gave me a ride, but then she disappeared to get her dog bathed, have her car worked on, show her bike to a prospective buyer, and do other important things. She assured me she would file a claim with her insurance company and help me financially.

Three days later, without consulting me, she called an ambulance and sent me back to the hospital, saying I had clostridium difficile (c-diff) a horrible intestinal bacterium one can get as a result of surgery. The emergency room doctor said I did not have it and sent me home. I called Bertha for a ride, but she did not answer. I called several times. I needed a ride, and Santa Fe did not have taxis, and there were no Ubers available.

I called a friend who was on her way to work and was driving close to my house. She checked the parking lot and reported that Bertha's trailer was gone; she had left town without telling me, leaving me stranded at the hospital. That friend came to the hospital and picked me up, making her late for work. I felt terrible, but there was nothing I could do. (I have since learned that an ambulance will take you home from the hospital if you do not have a ride.)

I was confined to a wheelchair for three months, unable to put any weight on that leg. Since I thought Bertha would be there, I did not have anyone scheduled to help me. I called the friend who was coming in two days from Phoenix and asked if she could come NOW. She hopped in her car and drove until late that night to get to my house.

I texted and called Bertha several times, but it was apparent that she was not going to return my calls. Over the next six months, I texted to let her know my progress but never received a response. And no offer of help from her or her insurance company ever came, as she had promised. It became evident that she was taking no responsibility and wanted nothing more to do with me. She had become a ghost in my life.

In today's world, where we live so far apart, it is easy to pretend people no longer exist, and things can be left dangling. In years gone by, everyone you knew lived in the same town, and you couldn't ghost someone as you were sure to run into them at the grocery store, church, or on the street.

I was not angry with Bertha for what happened, but it was tough to be abandoned at the hospital without a ride or someone to help me when I got home. Having the courage to face the situation must have been difficult since she never responded despite multiple opportunities.

Over the years, I have been sad to learn that those I thought were family or friends weren't. Just because they were important to me did not mean they felt the same. So, it was with Bertha. She was a biting ghost dog.

The Takeaway: Sometimes dogs just need to be muzzled.

Story 23
Life-Changing Dog

"Without change, there would be no butterflies."
HOLIDAY IN THE WILD

Every decision we make takes us down a different path or affirms the one we are on. One choice can set many changes in motion; even seemingly small decisions can have significant ramifications. The following account demonstrates how one choice I made created many changes in my life and the lives of those around me.

I had been married for 17 years when I realized it was time to end the marriage. There is no need to explain why, as it does not contribute to the story. I had three children who were also affected by my decision, and although it was hard, I knew it was the best thing to do. It was a life-changing experience that impacted our lives in many good ways, but it was not easy.

I had been devoted to my family and spent my days cooking, baking, cleaning, gardening, sewing doll clothes, working in my girls' classrooms, being a scout leader, taking kids to sporting events, and doing all the other things that go with being a mom. I supported the family when my husband was in college, but after he graduated, he said I could work if I wanted, but he would not help around the house. He made the choice easy; I stayed home with the children.

At the time of the divorce, we lived in Mission Viejo, California, and since I would now be the breadwinner, there was no way we could afford to stay there. I had been taking college and continuing education classes, which proved a blessing when we separated. One course was computer programming, which quickly translated to word processing. I went through that two-year program in two months and had a basis for work. I got a job with a prestigious real estate developer as their company's word processor, and the girls and I moved to Mountain View, California.

Learning my job, residing in a new area, living without a partner, and being a single parent to teenagers was a lot to manage. Along with these changes, I was having health issues. I also had to find service providers and make new friends. I had always trailed behind my husband and let him make introductions, but now I had to go up to strangers and introduce myself. And, of course, the girls were also facing their challenges. There were very few constants in our lives. All these major life shifts resulted from one decision—to leave my husband.

I knew things would be different by leaving, but I had no idea what they would be or feel like. I didn't know it then, but I got through those early days because I was naïve and numb. I got up each morning and did what was before me, putting one foot in front of the other. One doctor I saw for a physical issue told me I should see a therapist because of all the significant changes I had experienced; his wife just happened to be a psychiatrist. I thought he was either drumming up business for her, or perhaps he was the one who was nuts—I was doing just fine! I had dealt with tough situations my whole life, and this was just one more; I'd get through it.

I could have gone back to my ex-husband. He'd provide for our physical needs, but that was not all there was to consider. Yes, it was hard, but when I thought about how things would end if I returned to that relationship, I saw different ways our lives could go. None of them would have been easy, and the outcome would have been disastrous, especially for the children.

After considering both sides, I knew I had made the right choice. Since it was right, it would work out despite the difficult transition. Going back was not an option.

Getting a divorce was one of my life-changing dogs. We also create major changes when we buy a home, have a child, or take on new job responsibilities. Even if they are happy events, they can still be emotionally draining and stressful, causing us to feel overwhelmed and uncertain about the future. Sometimes, these experiences leave us questioning whether we made the right decision.

Besides the choices we make, there are some life-changing dogs that we would never consciously choose. These include an unexpected job loss, the death of a loved one, Alzheimer's, necessary relocation, life-threatening disease, earth disturbances, or unintended consequences of previous choices.

These differ from the dogs we have previously discussed because they are not just annoyances but significant, life-changing events. Our role in creating them can be less apparent, and they usually come as a shock, like a bomb being dropped.

Even though we may not consciously choose certain circumstances, everything happens for a reason. This sounds cliché, and it can be hard to see the good that can come from difficult times, especially when we're in the middle of them.

These things are threatening because we think we have little or no control. Realizing we have choices during a transition allows us to feel we do have some power. Using the runaway dog situation in "Story 1" as an example, let's explore some options for handling it.

1. We could wait for the commotion to settle before venturing out.
2. We could try yelling at the dogs to calm down.
3. We could stay in the house and play background music on the piano, like "Maple Leaf Rag."
4. We could run after the dog racing down the street, let someone else chase it, or wait for it to return.
5. We could ignore the chaos and continue what we are doing.
6. We could sit on the periphery and watch the drama unfold.

Every change presents new challenges, and knowing how to handle each requires a new approach. But taking a moment to pause and breathe can give us the clarity we need to make the best choice. We can find the right path forward with a calm mind and thoughtful consideration.

It's natural to feel unsure during the transition, but humans are resilient and can adapt and flourish in new situations once we get past the initial shock. With time and patience, we eventually settle into our new routine and wonder why we ever worried. Looking back, it may not have been comfortable, but we are different on the other side of change.

Life doesn't have to be difficult or full of suffering, but sometimes it feels that way, especially when we resist new circumstances. If we learn to embrace transition and approach it with an open mind and heart, we will find life easier to navigate.

Whether we knowingly or unknowingly attract change into our lives, it is there, and it is up to us to make the best of the situation despite our anger, fear, or aloneness. Trust yourself and recognize that you always have choices, even when dealing with life-changing circumstances. And remember, sometimes the answer may be to say, "This is not my dog."

The Takeaway: "It may be challenging some days, but if you are going to rise, you might as well shine."

UNKNOWN

Story 24
Not My Dog, But I Cried Anyway

"Since dogs live a week to one of our days,
they have to live fast."
NEIL DEGRASSE TYSON

Whether they are metaphorical or four-legged dogs, they have a way of sneaking into our lives. Some show up, others we choose, and others we inherit. No matter how they come to us, they are a gift, even if that is not obvious at the time.

If they have been a drain on our energy, we may be happy when they leave, but with others, it can be one of the most heartbreaking experiences we go through, making it incredibly difficult to let go. My friend Scott shared a story that highlights this point.

Dylan and I had been friends for years, so when he moved to town, it seemed logical that he would share my home in the historic district. In

116

addition to having my friend close by, I was re-modeling the house and could use his input.

I already shared my house with Ana, a beautiful Husky who had been my roommate since she was a puppy. I say "roommate" because she was not just my dog but my companion. Just days after Dylan moved in, Ana died; she would have been thirteen. It was one of the most significant moments that Dylan and I shared, that is, until Rune.

It was weirdly embarrassing that my dog died the first weekend he was there, and I became a puddle of tears. He sat with me and then helped load Ana's body into the truck so we could take her to the crematorium. She was not his dog, but he cried anyway.

Dylan wanted to get another dog, but I felt resistant. As we talked about it, memories of Jager flooded my mind. We had pet sat for him for nine months. Jager was a boxer, and he had issues! He needed more attention than the two of us could give him. I had never experienced anything like that, and when his owner returned *from active duty, Dylan and I sat on the front step anxiously waiting for him to reclaim his problem. Jager was not our dog!*

A year later, Dylan found Rune. Rune was a mixed-breed rescue dog who began life on the Pine Ridge Reservation in South Dakota. She found her way to the city through the Oglala Pet Project, which helps abused and abandoned animals from the reservation find a new life. She was sick and abused. The vet had to shave her because of various skin problems and infestations, but he declared her fit. He said she was about a year old.

When Dylan brought his hairless, shallow-bodied dog home, I wondered what he was thinking. But as I looked into Rune's eyes, they told me she had seen too much in her young life. Despite her shaky beginning, I saw the serenity and instantly felt what Dylan had.

At first, Rune was distant. Considering her history, we expected an adjustment period but wondered if she would ever trust us. We coaxed her to come to us. We took her outside and let HER lead US on a leash. It took about a month before she perked up. Then, one day, she realized she had hit the jackpot with her new people! She was safe. It was a total transformation; she became that one-in-a-million dog with a spectacular attitude and gentle playfulness.

Dylan loved that dog, and she went with him to work, hiking, and traveling. She delighted and comforted everyone who met her. As her body began to slow down, she developed an inoperable cyst that repeatedly ruptured. Her blood loss was extreme; Dylan felt he had lost her several times, only to have her perk back up a few days later. Eventually, it became apparent that her body could no longer support life and that the time had come.

Dylan found a vet service that would come to the house so her passing could happen in a place she knew and where she felt safe. I was with them in the backyard under the shade tree when the vet administered the sedative. She slipped out of her body in peace. As she took her last breath, she looked at us as if to say, "Thank you for my wonderful life." The serenity in her eyes comforted us.

And as Dylan had been with me when Ana passed, I was with him when his beloved Rune left her body. She was not my dog. But I cried anyway.

The dogs we meet may not be ours, but they can become part of our world when we least expect it. Our attachment develops, and we often don't even realize it is happening. Once a dog (four-legged or metaphorical) wriggles its way into our hearts, it is frequently hard to let it go, even if we know, "This is not my dog."

The Takeaway: It can surprise us when dogs become part of our lives.

Final Thoughts

"All growth starts at the end of your comfort zone."
                                                    TONY ROBBINS

Some people put much effort into finding the perfect dog that suits their personality and lifestyle. However, they often neglect to use the same level of discernment before accepting other things into their lives, like habits, relationships, or career paths. Choosing wisely can make life easier, but in a way, it doesn't matter because every experience, whether positive or negative, helps us grow and improve ourselves.

Both four-legged and metaphorical dogs teach us that setting boundaries is not unkind but rather a way of communicating what works and what doesn't. When things don't work, it doesn't mean they are necessarily wrong—they just don't suit us. We all have different needs and preferences, which is good to recognize.

It is not a cop-out to say no. So, before taking ownership of someone else's problem, ask yourself if it's really yours. Establishing clear and firm boundaries enables us to practice self-care, avoid conflicts, and help others understand how we wish to be treated.

If you have difficulty saying, "It's not my dog," here are other ways to say the same thing that may fit the situation better.

- I'm not the one who usually handles that.
- I'm not sure I can help.
- Not my circus, not my monkey.
- That's not my responsibility.
- I'm not the right person to do that.
- That has nothing to do with me.
- That falls outside my jurisdiction.
- I'm not in a place to handle that right now.

These statements put accountability for the situation back with the person it belongs to.

Taking on other people's problems was part of our identity in a bygone era, but that is over, and it is time for us to change that program. Most of the problems we hang onto are not ours, yet we cling to them because it is a chance to ignore our own issues, do good, or shine as someone's hero. However, it is more important that everyone face their challenges and become the hero of their story.

Being a hero means being courageous when things are hard. For some, it could be using their skills to save lives. For others, it could be trying something new like rock climbing, skydiving, or ice skating. Being a hero can also mean facing difficult situations like losing a child, dealing with a health issue, or testifying in court. In some cases, it could even be getting out of bed in the morning.

It's natural to want to help others during tough times, but we must remember that they are ultimately responsible for their own challenges. Trying to fix everything for everyone can lead to us being taken advantage of, leaving us feeling like doormats instead of heroes.

What you allow into your life is up to you. Use discernment and remember that whatever you choose comes with options, but they may not be apparent initially. That is when you step back, take a deep breath, and look at the situation objectively; you will know what to do.

Even if you end up with something that is not yours, it is okay because you learn the next time to say, "That is not my dog."

The Takeaway: You are perfect. Own who you are.

About the Author

Nancy DeYoung's love of writing began in second grade and never wavered. After high school, she attended college, majoring in communication, and that was where she met her husband, who received his degree in civil engineering. During their seventeen years of marriage, they had three daughters and lived and traveled to many cities and countries. After the children were grown and the husband was out of the picture, Nancy continued her travels.

Ms. DeYoung worked for a real estate development company for eight years. She later co-wrote Occupational Safety and Health Administration (OSHA) manuals for a fabrication company. Nancy is an avid journal writer and taught "Get a Grip: Get a Journal" classes for many years. She had four papers published in the International Association of New Sciences Proceedings. Her articles have appeared online and in many magazines. She has published three books: *Modern Shamans, Shaman's Vision*, and *The Girl in the Tent: Memoir from the Road*.

Nancy says, "I have always written and always will because there is so much to say. There may be a limited number of words in the English language, but there are a gazillion ways to put them together."